Heidi S.M.

SPIRIT OF
SPEYSIDE

HEIDI M. SANDS

First published in Great Britain in 2010

Copyright text and photographs © 2010 Heidi M. Sands

All rights reserved. No part of this publication may be reproduced, stored in a retrieval system, or transmitted in any form or by any means without the prior permission of the copyright holder.

British Library Cataloguing-in-Publication Data
A CIP record for this title is available from the British Library

ISBN 978 1 906887 77 3

PiXZ Books
Halsgrove House, Ryelands Industrial Estate,
Bagley Road, Wellington, Somerset TA21 9PZ
Tel: 01823 653777
Fax: 01823 216796
email: sales@halsgrove.com

An imprint of Halstar Ltd, part of the Halsgrove group of companies
Information on all Halsgrove titles is available at: www.halsgrove.com

Printed and bound in China by Toppan Leefung Printing Ltd

Introduction

Speyside is as diverse as it is interesting whether cloaked in winter splendour or summer beauty, and the jewel in its crown is the great River Spey itself.

Rising from the vicinity of little Loch Spey, at more than 300m, south of the Corrieyairack forest, 18 miles west of Newtonmore and 10 miles south of Fort Augustus, the power of the Spey begins. Running for just over 100 miles in length to Spey Bay on the coast, this most magnificent of salmon rivers diverts through heather hills, farmland and villages, skirting rocky outcrops, all the while swirling round and under a variety of bridges. It enhances the beauty of the natural environment and brings visitors into the area from across the world.

Amongst the most famous attractions on Speyside, within a stone's throw of the banks of the river itself, are some of the world's biggest and best malt whisky distilleries. With names such as the Macallan, the Aberlour and Glenfarclas this can truly be said to be 'The Spirit of Speyside'.

But that's not all that the area has to offer. Castles out of fairytales and history sit alongside churches of character. Local business rubs shoulders with international favourites, and wildlife, nature and native breeds mingle in this very special place.

Quite simply, Speyside has it all.

Ben Aigan winter snow scene.

Opposite page:
Ben Aigan winter sunshine.

Standing at the side of the road along which General Wade's troops passed en route from Strathspey to Fort Augustus, this disused farm bothy has seen better days but is remarkably well preserved.

Snow sculpture.

Woodland as old as the hills is a much
needed commodity on Speyside.

Alongside the River Spey a selection of handcrafted peeled bark sticks.

Opposite page:
The bones of the sea at Spey Bay.

Highland cattle in the snow.

The swing bridge over the Spey connecting Wester Elchies to Aberlour.

The Spey dam built to take water via a pipeline to the aluminium smelter at Fort William.

The Spey dam reservoir on the Alcan Estate 10 miles south west of Newtonmore.

The back of the Spey dam, an impressive sight.

Snow clearing on Speyside.

Opposite page:
Sheep near the Macallan distillery braving the snow.

Inveravon church Pictish warrior gravestones.

Inveravon church.

Washed up sea sculptures at Spey Bay.

Essential requirements alongside
the river at Aberlour.

Opposite page:
Fishing by Aberlour's
swing bridge.

At Dufftown this display leaves the visitor in no doubt as to the area's strong connection to the whisky industry.

Barrels for whisky fill the skyline at the cooperage at Craigellachie.

Lossiemouth on the periphery of Speyside.

The fairytale 1850s' Porters Lodge of Ballindalloch Castle.

Opposite page:
Ballindalloch Castle photographed from the top of the stunning rock garden.

The Linn Falls on the Lour Burn.

Opposite page:
Ruthven Barracks near Kingussie. The barracks were used to avoid
trouble after the 1715 Jacobite rebellion. Today they have a more
serene appearance standing guard over Insch marshes, a RSPB reserve.

Standing near the church the old railway station at
Aberlour is now the Speyside Way visitor centre.

The Spey at Aberlour.

Farming is an integral part
of Speyside life – here ploughing
goes on apace beside the river.

Dufftown Pipe Band piping a mounted cavalcade under the bridge by the Mash Tun public house in Aberlour. Local rider Miss A. Scott bears the Whisky Festival flag riding her own mount.

Opposite page:
Laggan stores the only shop for over 20 miles. It is stocked with just about everything you can think of from socks to peppermint tea.

Hill farming on Speyside.

The forwarder, a much
used machine in the
forestry industry
on Speyside.

Rothiemurcus Estate seen from Speyside with the Lairig Ghru
pass behind. The pass runs from Deeside to Strathspey and was once used as
a drove road. At its highest it reaches approximately 2733 feet.

Blacksboat Station along the Speyside Way.

Opposite page:
Loch Spey where the great river begins life. Seen here a June rainstorm
prepares to roll in across the Monadhliath Mountains.

An abandoned farmstead on moorland near Rothes contrasts with modern wind turbines in the background.

Pines on the Rothes Estate: forestry is important to the area's economy.

Once home to the Leslie family one wall is now all that remains of Rothes Castle that sits high above the Speyside village of the same name.

Broomhill Station where several scenes for the
popular TV series 'Monarch of the Glen' were filmed.

Glenfarclas still.

Etched by the winter
snows on Speyside.

Pitchroy Lodge home to Captain W.E. Johns from 1947 to 1953 – it was here
he wrote many of his world-famous Biggles novels right at the side of the Spey.

The bridge at Melgarve on the Corrieyairack Pass built by General Wade's troops in 1731, follows a track within a stone's throw of the infant Spey as it makes its way from Loch Spey.

Kirk Laggan bridge over the Spey – the original was designed by Thomas Telford, and as a result of a flood in 1825, this is all that remains.

Spey Bay where river meets the sea.

A winter wonderland.

A Speyside walk with rod and line.

Opposite page:
Derelict croft houses, often ruinous, litter the uplands of Speyside.

Badenoch and Strathspey's
Loch Morlich in the Glenmore
Forest Park, which ultimately
flows into the Spey via the Druie.

Where the Avon meets the Spey.

Thomas Telford's bridge famously spans the river at Craigellachie.
Built between 1812 and 1814 it was closed to road traffic in 1972.

Opposite page:
The Convals in the snow.

The dark peaty waters of the Spey are home to varied wildlife – here beneath the Telford bridge at Craigellachie a cormorant stretches its wings.

Red deer are often seen in the area. These sit in the winter sun
at Kingussie at the Highland Wildlife Centre.

Spring lambs populate farmland right across the area.

Opposite page:
Knockando church.

Seen from across Speyside the foothills of the Cairngorm
mountain range complete with summer snow.

Cairngorms National Park granite sign.

Tools of the fisherman's trade.

Opposite page:
The Crombie Burn as it passes the Scalan seminary at
the foot of the Ladder Hills at Glenlivet on Greater Speyside.

Village life – deep in conversation by the clock tower at Dufftown.

Opposite page:
A lone walker on the Speyside Way.

Speyside is cattle country – the ground being highly suitable for beef production.

Pretty as a picture — Archiestown village.

A single Tornado aircraft from Lossiemouth approaches Aberlour over the Spey as the annual Speyside Whisky Festival reaches its climax.

Opposite page:
Ben Rinnes dominates the skyline over much of central Speyside.

Taking a well earned rest – a walker on the Speyside Way at Aberlour.

The RAF Dallachy Strike Wing memorial at Bogmoor 2 miles from Spey Bay,
dedicated to those who flew against and destroyed German boats in the
North Sea and off the Norwegian coast between 1944 and 1945.

Spectacular Speyside sunset over Hunthill and farmland at Elchies.